READING POWER

Biomes

Deciduous Forests

Holly Cefrey

The Rosen Publishing Group's
PowerKids Press™
New York

Published in 2003 by The Rosen Publishing Group, Inc.
29 East 21st Street, New York, NY 10010

First Edition

Book Design: Mindy Liu

Photo Credits: Cover © James Randklev/Corbis; p. 4 (inset) © MapArt, graphic by Mindy Liu; pp. 4–5, 6 © David Muench/Corbis; p. 7 © Frank Blackburn, Ecoscene/Corbis; pp. 8, 11, 21 © Index Stock; p. 9 (top) Richard Shiell/Animals Animals; p. 9 (bottom) © Lynda Richardson/Corbis; p. 12 © Perry Slocum/Animals Animals; p. 13 © Charles Mauzy/Corbis; pp. 14–15 © Liz Hymans/Corbis; p. 17 © John Lemker/Animals Animals; p. 18 (inset) © Philip Gould/Corbis; pp. 18–19 © Nancy Rotenberg/ Animals Animals; p. 20 © Joel W. Rogers/Corbis

Library of Congress Cataloging-in-Publication Data

Cefrey, Holly.
Deciduous forests / Holly Cefrey.
    p. cm. — (Biomes)
Summary: Describes the fragile ecosystem of deciduous forests.
Includes bibliographical references (p.   ).
ISBN 0-8239-6454-X (lib. bdg.)
1. Forest ecology—Juvenile literature. [1. Forest ecology. 2. Ecology.] I. Title.
QH541.5.F6 C34 2003
577.3—dc21
                                    2002000104

Contents

Deciduous Forests

Deciduous forests are found mainly in North America, Europe, and Asia. These forests have four seasons—winter, spring, summer, and fall. Most of the trees in a deciduous forest lose their leaves in the fall.

■ Deciduous forest

4

Now You Know

A biome *(BY-ohm)* is a plant and animal community that covers a large part of the earth.

By losing their leaves, the trees in a deciduous forest are able to live through cold winters. If the leaves stayed on the trees in the winter, they would freeze. Icy leaves would weigh branches down, making the branches snap and break off the trees. In the spring, the trees grow new leaves.

In the fall, the leaves of deciduous trees change color.

Now You Know

Deciduous comes from the Latin language and means "to fall off."

Layers of the Forest

A deciduous forest is made up of five different layers. The layers are called canopy, understory, shrub, herb, and floor. Each layer has different plants and animals living in it.

The branches and leaves of the tallest trees make up the canopy. Trees of the canopy receive the most sunlight. Birds that eat fruit live in the canopy. Insects and mammals that eat leaves or fruit also live in the canopy.

In thick forests, leaves only grow at the tops of trees.

Virginia creeper vine

Vines, such as the Virginia creeper, grow in the canopy. Flowers and fruit on the vines become food for birds and other animals.

Barred owls nest in the canopy layer of deciduous forests.

9

Young trees, small trees, and plants make up the understory. These trees and plants grow well without much light. They have broad, flat leaves. The leaves help the plants catch the sunlight that is not blocked by the canopy. Some of these plants lose their leaves each year.

Dogwoods, which grow in the understory, have beautiful flower blossoms each spring.

The shrub layer is home to many birds and insects. Shrubs have woody stems like trees. However, they usually have more than one stem and do not grow as large as trees.

The blue jay lives in the deciduous forest. It drops oak seeds from the forest onto farm fields. The seeds grow into trees.

Rhododendrons are shrubs that grow in the deciduous forest. They keep their leaves all year long.

Ferns, grasses, wildflowers, and very young trees make up the herb layer. Forest animals that live on the ground, such as mice, snakes, bears, and deer, make their home here.

The ground of the forest makes up the floor. The floor is covered by leaves, twigs, and other things that fall from higher layers.

Indian paintbrush and sunflowers grow in the herb layer of deciduous forests. The soil of the floor is made richer by these wildflowers when they die.

Forest Soil

The rich soil of deciduous forests helps new plants and trees to grow. The soil is made healthy by the rotting bodies of dead animals and dead plants. Some animals, such as worms, break down the dead animals and plants.

Fungi

Bacteria, earthworms, fungi, and spiders help break down dead plants and animals.

People and the Forest

People use the deciduous forest in many ways. They use the wood from trees to make paper, plastics, and cloth. People also build their homes with the wood from the deciduous forest. In many places, wood is used for cooking and heating, too.

Wood from deciduous forests is taken to factories, where it can be made into paper.

Deciduous forest plants and trees, like all green plants, give off oxygen and add to our air supply. Forests also soak up extra rainwater, preventing floods. Without the forests, many kinds of plants and animals could not live. The deciduous forest biome is important to many forms of life.

People have reduced the forests from one-half of Earth's surface to one-third. When forests are destroyed, many plants and animals that live there are hurt.

Many people enjoy the beauty of deciduous forests.

Glossary

bacteria (bak-**tihr**-ee-uh) very tiny living things; some are useful, while others cause sickness

canopy (**kan**-uh-pea) the highest part of a forest that is made up of the tops of tall trees

deciduous forest (dih-**sihj**-oo-uhs **for**-ihst) a forest where most trees lose their leaves each fall

fungi (**fuhn**-jy) living plantlike things that have no leaves, flowers, or green coloring

herb (**erb**) small, soft-stemmed plants, many of which are used for medicine and food seasonings

layer (**lay**-uhr) one thickness or level of something that is on top of another

shrubs (**shruhbz**) low, bushy plants

stems (**stehmz**) the parts of a plant that hold the leaves

understory (**uhn**-duhr-stor-ee) the layer in a deciduous forest where small animals, plants, and young trees live and grow

Resources

Books

Temperate Deciduous Forest
by April Pulley Sayre
Twenty-First Century Books (1995)

A Walk in the Deciduous Forest
by Rebecca L. Johnson
Carolrhoda Books (2000)

Web Sites

Due to the changing nature of Internet links, PowerKids Press has developed an online list of Web sites related to the subjects of this book. This site is updated regularly. Please use this link to access the list:

http://www.powerkidslinks.com/bio/dcd/

Index

Word Count: 453

Note to Librarians, Teachers, and Parents

If reading is a challenge, Reading Power is a solution! Reading Power is perfect for readers who want high-interest subject matter at an accessible reading level. These fact-filled, photo-illustrated books are designed for readers who want straightforward vocabulary, engaging topics, and a manageable reading experience. With clear picture/text correspondence, leveled Reading Power books put the reader in charge. Now readers have the power to get the information they want and the skills they need in a user-friendly format.